KING ALFRED'S COLLEGE
WINCHESTER

To be returned on or before the day marked
below :—

PLEASE ENTER ON ISSUE SLIP:

AUTHOR   DE GRAFT

TITLE   Beneath the jazz and brass

ACCESSION No.   99421

AFRICAN WRITERS SERIES

166

BENEATH THE JAZZ AND BRASS

Beneath the Jazz and Brass

J. C. DE GRAFT

LONDON
HEINEMANN
NAIROBI · IBADAN · LUSAKA

Heinemann Educational Books Ltd
48 Charles Street, London WiX 8AH
PMB 5205 Ibadan · PO Box 45314 Nairobi
PO Box 3966 Lusaka
EDINBURGH MELBOURNE AUCKLAND
TORONTO HONG KONG SINGAPORE
KUALA LUMPUR NEW DELHI

ISBN 0 435 90166 4

Set in Monotype Baskerville and
Printed in Great Britain by
Cox & Wyman Ltd, London, Fakenham and Reading

CONTENTS

3   SOMETHING IN THE SKY

To the memory of
Mary Smith, whom we all called Mena;
Kweku Joe, whom we all called Papa; and
Janet Acquaye – Mame:
My mother of the tears
And my sustainer through the years,
Single among all women
Rare bead that speaks not . . .

I

SILVER DEWDROPS AND GOLDEN SHADOWS

Smiling Baby

Little baby boy nestling cosy
Among your soft pillows,
May it be you know?
Your mother knows, though she never tells it.
And perhaps one day
When you are old enough
You also will know – if already
The winds that come breezing in through your window
And the little sparrows that come chip-chirping on the sill
Have not whispered it into your little ears.
You will not be happy then, little boy;
Maybe you'll sigh and wish you never had been born,
You little bastard baby boy.

They little thought of you then, bastard boy,
Little your mother and father thought of you
That moment somewhere –
Perhaps in some cheerless, stale, ill-furnished,
In-hemmed piece of veranda-bed-sitting-room
Somewhere, somewhere. . . .
(No, we never do, we never think of others
Those moments supremely good or evil
When we identify ourselves to the hilt with
Life the Maker,
Muscle and nerve in passion buckled,
Rhythm-driven and suspended in rhythm:
No, we never do. . . .
It's always ourselves we think of
If we think at all then) –
Little they thought of you as they forged you
On anvil of muscle and nerve,
Poor little bastard baby boy.

[2]

And when the anvil cooled
And these little limbs waxed hard inside your mother,
He forsook her – yes, your father did –
He forsook her, would not take her,
Spat and swore he never knew her!
So she came weeping to her people,
Weeping that she'd been betrayed,
Bearing the secret of you inside her,
Paling and sickening as the moons filled and leaned;
Till with the ninth moon it came,
Her dear secret came sneezing out –
And it was you,
You, poor little bastard baby boy.

Ah, you smile, baby boy!
But you smile only because you do not know:
To know is not to smile,
For knowledge is darkness, and
Night drives out the day!
So smile while yet there is light,
Smile,
My poor little bastard baby boy.

April 1955

[3]

Lull-a-Dirge

Don't cry, baby,
Sleep, little baby;
Father will nurse you,
Sleep, baby, sleep.

Lonely bird flitting away to the forest so fast,
Gold-speckled finch, your feathers wet all fading,
Tell me, shivering bird, have you seen her –
Have you seen my crying baby's mother?

> She went to the river at early dew,
> A pot upon her head;
> But down the water floats her pot,
> And the path from the river is empty.

Shall I take him under the palm
Where the green shade rests at noon?
> Oh no, no, no,
> For the thorns will prick my baby.

Shall I take him under the giant bombax
Where the silk-cotton plays with the wind?
> Oh no, no, no,
> For the termite-eaten bough will break
> And crush my little baby,
> My little sleeping baby.

The day is long and the sun grows hot,
So sleep, my little baby, sleep;
For mother is gone to a far, far land – alas!
She is gone beyond the river!

Signals Road, March 1963

[4]

The Cage

Once upon a time I caught a dove.
Swinging high ten branches up
Where the blue winds swept the skies,
High up above the dizzy leaves
I caught her as she came to rest,
My young heart fluttering.

In a rusty cage I mewed her up
And all morning dreamed for her
A house of gold and silver wire
Where she might coo forever
To my heart that fluttered
As I watched her restless eyes,
Watched in wonder through her bars.

But oh, she flew away,
My downy-breasted little dove;
At height of noon she flew away
When to her cage I brought her
Fresh grains of milky maize
And sugared water in a cup;
Out of her cage she sprang and
Off over my head was gone!

Dove cooing in your tree
High up, at sunset cooing,
My heart is numb with weeping
For your sister I lost at noon.
When morning comes again
Will my cage be empty still?
Or will my lost love return
To set a-flutter
Once again
My earth-bound heart
    Watching her through my bars?

Signals Road, 16 July 1962
Nairobi, 22 April 1973

Melancholic Reciprocal

Hidden thorns quiver in your cheeks
On your brow the shadow of lingering sorrow.

Melancholy one,
When unfulfilled longings stir
    Round your navel
And tears well up, blinding,
Remember –

        I too have known
        The fresh morning mist's caress,
        When blossoming orchids held the world's
                heart of splendour;
        Known too, like you,
        The thrill of a mother's answering laughter,
        Hope in the flutter of a swallow's wing.

Remember me,
Orphan girl weeping at the stream.

Legon, 30 October 1966

Footsteps

TO L.

Five o'clock.
Footsteps on the veranda –
Clear, ringing steps
Light and thrilling.

I see them: shapely little feet;
They come tap . . . tap . . . tapping
Nearer and nearer
Upon the cement floor,
Upon the threshold of my heart.

Dainty little feet
In little black suede shoes,
High heels not so high,
Erect without effort.

I feel them: steady little feet;
They come pat . . . pat . . . patting
Along the strings of my heart,
Deeper and deeper
Into my lonely life.

Little feet, I cannot stop you;
Little feet, *Akwaaba!*

South West, May 1951

Sea Love

In the broiling heat of the noon-day sun
There stood a youth mending his net;
And as he deftly threw his shuttle
He crooned in tenor deep and low:

    The fish I always longed to catch
    I never caught
    I never caught;
    The fish I always longed to eat
    Would never take my bait;
    But now I've got myself a net
    And bought myself a new canoe
    Beware!
    You cheeky little fish
    Beware!

And as he swiftly pulled the knot
He sang, his voice vibrating low:

    O-o-o-oh,
    I've got me more than a hook –
    Beware!

In the noon-day shade of her palm-wine shed
There sat a maiden on a stool;
With a twig from a broom she picked her tooth,
And as she listened to the youth
She smiled – a sly and knowing smile.

The maiden chuckled to herself
And sucked her tooth so you could hear;
She pulled her cloth around her knees
She drew the folds into her lap
Then sang – a naughty twinkle in her eye,
Her rich contralto charged with sauce:

    The sea is wide
    The sea is deep
    The sea is green and dark below;
    Come all canoes
    Come all your nets
    There'll still be nooks
    Secure from hooks
    For little fish to stow.

Quick she flipped into her lap
The folds of cloth still hanging free;
Quick snapped her knees together shut –
Her full contralto calling low:

    Go-o-o-oh,
    If you long for fish to eat,
    Go, eat your mother!

May 1962

Akosua 'Nowa

They say the guinea-fowl lays her treasure
Where only she can find it.
Akosua 'Nowa is a guinea-fowl;
Go tell her, red ant upon the tree.

I met Akosua 'Nowa this morning;
I greeted:
      Akosua, how is your treasure?
She looked me slowly up and down,
She sneered:
      The man is not yet here who'll find it!

Akosua 'Nowa has touched my manhood;
Tell her, red ant upon the tree:
If she passes this way I am gone,
I am gone to load my gun.

No matter how hidden deep her treasure,
By my father's coffin I swear
I'll shoot my way to it this day;
Son of the hunter king
    There is liquid fire in my gun!

Legon, 8 March 1967

Uneasy Engagement

You wear a look upon your face
    I do not understand:
Neither of pleasure nor displeasure,
Yet decidedly not calm –
    As if some recent memory
    Still lingered painfully sweet on your mind
    Making it unsure
    Whether to treasure or reject my love.
Or is it because I wondered aloud a moment ago
    Whose shadows they might have been
    Slinking into deeper shadow
        Behind the bougainvillaea
    When I called to see you yesternight?
        An unwitting question, I own,
        Which please, my dear, forgive me. . . .

Your old man was sure you were up in your room
And would have gladly called you downstairs, good fellow,
    Had I not pleaded kindness
    To my tired fiancée sleeping. . . .

But that giggling as I left,
That giggling from behind the bougainvillaea,
    Loud ringing in my twice-made-sensitive ears
    Like altar bells out of time with the service –
Some maiden's, perhaps, killed with stolen kisses?
        You think not so, I see
        From your shy averted eyes. . . .

Anyhow –
    Whatever it was that made her giggle
        (Whoever she might be)
    I pray the stars 'twas no more than a tickle
    Administered by her companion
    In celebration of his luck
        (Or triumph, depending how he felt)
    That I was so infatuated
        (Or so just-plain-idiotic)
    As to whistle out your name
    Approaching your father's enshadowed gate.

Legon, 25 July 1968

The Poem I Cannot Write

I would mould a poem
          about you,
Only
      Words snap in the shaping
      Too brittle–coarse to take your form
          The mystic serenity of you
So I am left with the memory of
      A lady giving alms –
          Vision of grace
             among beggars –
Inimitable you
      Giving alms.

Legon, 4 April 1968

Resurrection

I dreamed of a world dead and dying;
The fiery firmament – suns and stars –
All to cinder dying;
Forests once fecund,
All animate things, excepting you and me,
All dead;
And there was no sea.

But in the glooming grey,
As I focused you through my tears
I knew,
Deep in my loin I knew
That all was not forever lost.

They say that out of heavenly harmony
God the Maker framed this universe;
But from the ashes of this nightmare waste
Shall rise another world,
Quickened by the light from your eyes
And the tender warmth of your smile.

Signals Road, 27 June 1963

[15]

The Canary

On the rocky bank of a waterless stream
I sat beneath a lime tree,
And the bitter thirst rose to my heart.

Then suddenly
I heard a singing in the air and,
Up-glancing,
Saw you perched upon a branch.

My rinsed heart overflows with your song
Soothing as virgin water from the skies.

28 June 1963
Nairobi, 22 April 1973

A Dream of Lovers Meeting

With trembling lips I grope
For you;
I reach out my tongue
Still seeking you;
Then I find you
Suddenly
And we meet
    Hang together
        Swaying as in a swell –
            Cling like twins drowning. . . .

I gasp
    I flounder
        I sink
            Dying to your soft murmurs. . . .
And wrapped up in your brooding warmth
I wonder where . . . where . . . ?

Slowly the dream disperses,
But still I feel you there
Smiling down at me:
Your face
    Your brows
        Your eyes –
Tender as breezes at evensong
    Calm as hills after a storm
        Mysterious as a tropic night in full moon.

N.H., 8 October 1960

The Dance (1)

Kick up your chin and laugh –
    You
    Whoever you may be
    My partner in the dance –
Kick up your chin and laugh;
For though the squint-eyed owl screeches,
The plummeting seagulls will
        Rise again
            And circle with us
    While we two dance.

Look –
Three holy faces
Sneering up from the shimmering bed of the dry pond;
Look now –
Countless water weeds and lilies
Swaying in the rising ripples,
And silvery fish quick-darting
And golden fish frisking after
    As we two dance.

Home . . . turn . . .
    Arms akimbo
Two-three, two-three . . .
    Arms akimbo
Flexing torsos . . .
    Arms akimbo
Rippling muscles . . .
    Arms akimbo
Thumping throb of lifting feet –
Ours the riddle of the dance.

The fountain splashes the cobbles wet
And the moon discovers her mate
    In crevice pools:
Ours the message
    Of the swivelling constellations
Ours the pattern
    Of the seasons.

Kick up your chin and laugh.
For we know
    By the surge of the drum plasma
    In the vessels of our heart
When the twin-timpani thunder –
We know
    (man and woman made he us)
Ours is the mystery of the dance,
Ours the mastery
    Of death.

October 1964

Daemonic Love

You took my man away;
In the mid-bloom of my marriage morn
You took my man away.

When I came questing at your door
You had him yoked in honey toil
When I came questing at your door.

You turned your lock upon my face
And sneered he shall not come to me,
You turned your lock upon my face;

And –

He laughed I would not come again,
The love-pang twisting at my heart
He laughed I would not come again.

I have been on a long, long journey;
I have been among the northern hills
Where the red god broods in his cave:
I have been among the hills of Tongo.

Though you possess my man every hour,
His soul that I have drunk
In three draughts with white kola
Deep in the caves of Tongo –
That cannot you possess,
Not if you sprout ten thousand talons
To clutch him to your breast.

And –

Oh he shall come to me
And I shall receive him
Not once nor seventy times,
But whenever in the hold of your grasping love-lips
The wild shudders shake him:
'Tis me shall receive his liquid ecstasies –
Me you sneered away in the morning,
Me
His woman returned from Tongo.

1 June 1965

Platinum Lou

You'll come, won't you?
Come at seven and meet my wife –
    Plenty to drink
    And talk of good old days.

So we trooped in at seven expecting Sam
    Of old –
    Gay.

Come in, boys – and girls, right in:
    Small-dee and John and Ofori and Kobina
    And John's wife Mansa and Ofori's Elsie;
Here's Lou, my wife:
    We met in college – Columbia;
    She's a peach ain't she?

And such a wife!
    Radiant as a Madison Avenue debutante,
    Shop-window legs and
    Swooning bust and, jeez,
    What a crown of dazzling hair!

Take it easy, folk, this is home.

So we relaxed.
    Lou shook us cocktails –
    East-coast mixtures richly blooming;
    Sam held her elbow and
        Afterwards
            Served the drinks.

We talked and drank
We drank and ate
    Dainty choppies.
The evening rolled on
    We rolled the floor away.
The highlife was good
    So was the jazz;
        And we danced
        To many tapes. . . .

        While Lou killed us
            With sophistication.
Have some more,
            Won't you?
Bourbon?
        Try it – wonderful!
Soda?
      Oh no, best on the rocks!
Or would you rather this *and* that
    or that
        or that
            or that
                or that?
Oh yes, do try a bit of that, it's good!
    Straight from the States –
        Friends of ours, you know,
        The embassy, you know,
        Simply good, man, good!

Sam sat and drank
    Spoke little
    Gazed through the window
    While Lou sparkled.

    [23]

And we –
We danced many a highlife
Which we –
We chased home with many a highball.

But Sam sat and drank
    Spoke little.
Marriage had come like a castrating angel flashing
    A platinum sword;
And Sam was subdued.

    We left them at the door
    Holding hands,
    His gaze at the receding stars.
    The early moon had set.

He will go in and clean up our mess –
    Mess left behind by
    Rowdy ghosts
    Conjured up from a youthful past
        By an unwitting invitation.

    And they will retire.
    And tomorrow
    After the thousandth mating session
        In fifteen years –
She all antiseptically prepared
And he hermetically sealed up in *durex*
        (under duresse) –
    Sam will wake up no whit nearer
    His dream of a bouncing piccaninny,
        And lap up his milk and honey
        Presented on the dot
        In choicest transatlantic chinaware.

[24]

And since his leave is still office fresh
    He'll curl up in the settee
    And read his *Time Magazine* just
        delivered from the States,
    Daring no venture into the tempting
        world of his kinswomen
        (Black whores!)
    An aged man in his middle prime.

Oh Sam, our Sam,
    Tell us, old Sam
        (or whisper if you will):
        Where the gaiety
        The old rumbustious gaiety?
        Where did you shed yourself?

    Dare we ask her
    Dare we, Sam,
    Dare we ask your platinum wife
        From New Orleans?

Legon, 5 June 1967

The Long Wait

Silver dewdrops sparkling in the sunrise
Budding dimples smiling in the dawn:

Tell me, good mother, tell me
Who shall my husband be?

Prince shall he be and handsome,
Feet befitting golden sandals,
Chaplet on his brow of camel weave,
And he shall come in the prime of noon.

Golden shadows racing in the sunset
Wispy tresses trembling in the dusk:

Sigh not, lonely heart, sigh not
The day will soon be gone.

I've waited and waited and waited
Till my eyes begin to droop;
Now my prince comes o'er the horizon
And at my door
Death's decked palanquin.

Legon, 15 December 1966

2

THIS SHRINE OUR POT

Not Ours the Pride

And Nyankopon said: Let there be rain. Let my spirit descend
    upon the earth in rain, to sustain my people.
And the people said: Wherewith shall we catch Nyankopon's
    spirit descending upon the earth in rain to sustain us?
And Nyankopon said: Make you sweet pots of the earth's clay
    to catch my rain, my spirit that shall sustain you.
So the people of all climes set about making sweet pots of the
    earth's clay to catch Nyankopon's spirit. . . .

But who shall knead our clay
To build our pot?
    What hands
    What pressure
    Of what hands
Knead this piece of the earth?
Clay mined from all rivers
Waters of man's rivers
That flow
From immemorial dawns.

        Behold the clay
        Won from man's rivers;
        But the kneading *our* task,
        The kneading *our* task.

Who shall mould this clay
To make our pot?
    What fingers
    What rhythm
    Of what fingers
Mould this piece of the earth?
Living clay
Rich with the virtue of many strains,
Virgin
Despite the rape of many winds.

[29]

Behold the clay
Rich with the goodness of many strains;
But the moulding our pride,
The moulding our pride.

Who shall pinch this clay,
Stipple-trim-tattoo our pot?
What nails
What pricking
Of what nails
Cicatrize this piece of the earth?
Sacred clay
Hallowed clay
Inmixed with the marrow
Of our fathers' bones.

Behold the clay
Textured with ancestral marrow;
So the pinching our birthright,
The pinching our birthright.

And who shall fire this clay
To temper our pot?
What shoulders
What power
Of what shoulders
Bring to the flame this piece of the earth?
Or who shall smoke this clay
To sweeten this pot?
This pot that shall catch
Nyankopon's spirit from the sky
To sustain this thirsty people?

[30]

This is our pot
This is our pot;
The firing *our* duty,
The smoking *our* duty.

How dare we name this pot our own
If other fingers
    Knead
    Mould and
    Pinch
The clay of its making?
If other hands
    Stipple-trim-tattoo
    Cicatrize
    Temper and
    Smoke
This shrine our pot?

Not ours then the pride
    Brother
Nor ours then the joy
    Sister
If other hands achieve
    O my people
If other hands achieve
    For us.

Legon, 16 February 1965
Nairobi, June 1971

City on an Anthill*

We raised a house
    Upon an anthill.
As the years passed it grew –
    A village, then a town
    Assuming pride of place among the
        townships of the land,
    Attracting hordes
Till soon we had
    A city on a dunghill.

They say
    A man does not point with his left finger
        at his mother's humble hut.
Must I then be muzzled?
Say, hovering vultures,
Must I then desist from singing
    This dunghill wreathed in bunting,
    This prince of squalid cities?

Legon, 20 January 1967

* There is a legend that Accra started as a settlement
among anthills.

Promoters of Culture

They entreated him
     To go and read them of his poetry;
     He went.
He bled them his heart
     Recalling his agonies in song:
     He wept.
Then from where he stood upon the dais
He saw them changing money at the door,
And he said to them:
          Must these people pay
          To share my sorrows?
          My tears are not for sale.
And smiling they replied:
               We know,
               Nor did we mean you injury;
               But where has it been heard before
               That the poet ceased from giving
               And we from taking?

Legon, 22 December 1968

Mother, give us Pause from the Frenzy

Mother,
We come to you with aching feet
    Feet that have danced through the centuries
    Without stop without change of pace,
And our voices are hoarse from singing to the drums
    Without stop without change of pitch.

Take pity on us
Mother;
Give us pause for a while
    From the frenzy of the drumming and the dancing
        Even though they be in praise of
        Your glory among the mothers of five continents;
Give us pause for thought,
    For the earth has moved past the rains,
    And the sowing already much delayed
        Because
            Intoxicated with the rhythm of the drums
        We danced and sang
           While others tilled *their* land.

Give us pause for thought,
Mother,
For the walls our fathers built now crumble to the ground
    And we have raised no fresh foundations
        Although we have not ceased from breeding;
The roofs have sprung a hundred leaks,
    Nor have we made new thatch
        Although there is no lack of grass;

The rafters trickle down to dust with beetles
    Because we have not tended them;
        And now
The ancestral drums crack!
The drums our fathers bequeathed to us
        Crack! –
    Their membranes worn thin
    Because we play them
        Without understanding
        Without inspiration;
    And their rhythms no longer communicate
        Life to our numbed feet
        Surge to our flagging voices;
And we have not made new drums.

Give us pause for thought,
Mother;
For though these aliens homeward bound
        From wandering the world
    Stop here for a while
    To marvel at our *innocence* –
        The while you proudly urge us on
        To drum and dance with more abandon –
Surely must you know,
Mother,
    That we cannot survive the coming seasons
        Our work of sowing still undone
        The old homes collapsing
        And no time for us
        To think about the changing times.

Give us pause in silence,
Mother,
    Each man with himself
        Away from the drunken crowd
        Away from the noise of the cracked drums
            that have lost their message;
    To ponder
        The challenges of the coming days,
    To discover
        New sources of strength
        For our exhausted feet and voices.

And, O Mother Africa
When the drums sound again
    May they be drums
        New-sculptured by *these* hands, not our fathers',
        Membraned with the skin of elephants
            We ourselves have hunted,
        Their rhythms and their message more meaningful
            Because textured from the fabric
            Of *our* life and aspirations;
May they sound in concert
        With instruments more subtly melodious,
        Voices new-charged with hope
            Of harvests
            Our reward for thoughtful labour;
And when we dance again
    Let us dance upon aspiring feet
        Youthful dances free and limber
        Flowing with the promise of the coming years.

But first,
O Mother,
Give us pause for thought,
Give us pause from the frenzy of the cracked drums.

Legon, 23 June 1968

Those were days
    When we went forth with thirsting heart
    Seeking along lonely valleys for springs
        That flow from ancient hills;
And having found a trickle, was it not joy
        To kneel
        And sip
        A few cool drops –
        Life to our wilting souls!
    Then was it reward enough but to labour
        In this quest,
    Then was it honour too.

But now –
    This picking of poor men's brains to sell
        as one's own for the highest bid on
        the American Grants market,
    And this desecration of holy shrines, eaves-
        dropping on the conversation of gods;
    This predacity,
        This hogging of every new talent that shows
        its golden face above the soil of Africa,
    Or this heady exaltation of every hunk of turd
        dropped by an African cow;
    This hurry and flurry up and down, nest-building
        and nest-feathering on other men's
        account,
    And this murderous competition for shares in
        the pan-Africanist industry –

If this be the end of all our search for Africa,
    Then,
You gods of our mothers' fathers,
    Forgive us,
    Forgive us
        Though deep in our breast
        We know what wrong we do.

Legon, 25 September 1967

The Multi-Messiah

The multi-messiah comes.
He is a creature of men.
    Beware the multi-messiah!

Men of feeble mind shall make a multi-messiah
    So that out of a million feeble minds may emerge
    One strong mind.
Beware them: they shall be strong.

Men of aspiring will shall make a multi-messiah
    So that out of a hundred aspiring wills may emerge
    One dominant will.
Beware them: they shall be dominant.

The multi-messiah knows no failure:
    Is he not alone panacea to every
    Social ill?
He is omniscient: mistrust him.

The multi-messiah brooks no opposition:
    Is he not alone master of every
    Situation?
He is omnipotent: disobey him.

The multi-messiah rules forever:
    Is he not the final choice of free people
    Bonded
In the exercise of their democratic rights?

He is power without remission
The one and only ruling party
The supreme will of the crowd
    Incarnate in one man:

Twice beware the multi-messiah.

Legon, 29 April 1968

The Signature

O life,
O limitless possibilities!
To think there ever could have been a break like that
    For me,
    ME!
But fate moves along mysterious byways
Her pleasure to fulfil;
And how I wish that all those sceptics had been there
    To see me in my glory . . .
        As if the gods in retaliation spoke
        At last!

Happy the man who arrives
    At the heights;
But happier he who
    Like me
Can *dunce* it still higher to

THE TOP!
    London:
    Whitehall:
    Gleaming conference table
        Reflecting chandeliers a-glitter
        On a late autumn afternoon;
    Mature oaken wainscotting, stained glass windows,
    Cavernous fire-place where burned
        A fire without a wisp of smoke;
    Red carpet, and plush on ancient princely chairs,
        And –
    Muted consultations among secretaries grey
        That tiptoed in and out as if on angel feet.

Sir James Willoughby, my opposite number
    (Of international law fame),
    Sat at the head of the table
    Flanked by his advisers –
        The Eminent Six,
        Terror of World Bank economists;
    And at this end,
    Immaculate in three-piece suit
        (Navy-blue)
        And silken tie to match
        (Spotted, and specially delivered from New York)
    Sat your friend –
    ME:
        Leading delegate of our great Republic,
            Representing no less an one than
            His Messianic Dedication Himself:
            Winner of Lost Battles
            Charging Elephant of the West!

Unlike our drafting sessions
And the tedious consultations
The ratification ceremony itself was brief,
The opening speeches briefer.

The pen they gave me was pure silver
    (Which I still keep – Care to have a look? –
    A fitting souvenir).
And when the long awaited moment came
    Despite the chill that trickled down my spine
        I signed
            X
    Right on . . . the dotted line

[43]

As each parchment copy came
    (Borne by a colonel in livery)
On a purple cushion embroidered in thread of gold with
    A crown
And underneath it, in curling letters,
        ER.

Six times I signed
    As instructed by the colonel –
    Ponsonby, a grand fellow,
    Late of the colonial service.

Did I hear you say something?
    The value – what do you mean *the value*?
You mean . . . Oh yes, of course . . .
    Eight-hundred-twenty-million cedis
    Of the old Republic's mineral and agricultural pro-
    ducts. . . .
        (*Wealth in sweat and raw materials*,
        According to that cheeky boy,
        That – that cheeky twerp!)

Did you say *for what*?
    Well, how do I know?
    For aid, of course:
        They were offering us good aid;
    That's why we had to do our best
        To put them at their ease.

What do you mean by *details*?
    I did not study the documents. . . .
    And why the bloody hell
        Should I have studied any document?
    That was clearly not my brief –
    My instructions were to sign!

Hunh?!
Of course, we had instructions
And more besides, all typed and neatly held in files:
    Full notes on the original drafts,
    Ministerial minutes and
    Central Committee memoranda –
    The lot!
But in London
    We couldn't find those files!
        Some incompetent chap or other
        Had forgotten, no doubt, to put them
        In the bag with our kenkey.
    Frantic telex calls back home
    Simply yielded no result;
    Yet luck was on our side –
        What with the copy of the *British notes*
        Our *English* back-room boys obtained for us,
        Just how I do not know.
Anyway. . . .

What – *my colleagues*?
　　Hopeless bunch of fellows: they did not have a clue!
　　　　Seven officers in all –
　　　　From the Attorney-General's,
　　　　Foreign Affairs and the H.C. –
　　　　For five days
　　　　They floundered round the clock
　　　　Trying to decipher (as they importantly put it)
　　　　　　The British notes
　　　　'So that we might be in a strong position
　　　　To negotiate favourable terms.'

But I tell you, brother,
Those British are unbeatable!
　　　　In such circumstances
　　　　What else could I have done to save my face?
　　　　So I decided on quick action
　　　　As leader of the delegation
　　　　　　Come life or instant death:
　　TO SIGN!

No opposition, you say?
No opposition!
　　　　Which brings me back once more
　　　　To that cheeky little fellow,
　　　　That whipper-snapper of a boy
　　　　Attached to us from the High Commission
　　　　　　To carry our despatches:
　　　　He insisted – would you believe it! –
　　　　That we must include a six-month review clause,
　　　　Which the British would not have – who would?

Oh yes, you're right:
It was indeed a tough assignment. . . .
　　　　[46]

But that boy. . . .
Anyway the British,
    At my firm intervention,
    Settled for twenty-four;
And that's how we won the day!

Afterwards came the toasts
And warm handshakes all round –
    Very amiable chaps, I can tell you,
    Sir James and the Eminent Six.
Whence,
    To cut a long story short,
By Rolls Royce they whisked us off to our Hotel
    To a sumptuous banquet in the evening
    And a wallowing night
    All laid on T.D.B.!
    (They certainly understand how to do these things,
    You know;
    The British, of course – who do you think I mean?)

But really,
To think there could have been a day
    Like *that*
    For me,
    ME,
    Once the dumb despair of teachers!
But even a dunce must have his day,
    Or don't you so concede?
And I can assure you
    It did feel good
    To score top mark at last!

    Nairobi, 19 August 1972

[47]

The Rock Behind the Fort

Under the eaves of the filling station
    A lunatic escaped from the asylum snores gently,
    Double-bent in sleep like a broken lobster;
Two prostitutes drift homewards,
    Misty with fatigue
    Musky with many males;
A tattered watchman on his rounds,
    His smoky lantern swaying,
    Returns to his dew-sodden mattress
    In the shadow of the warehouse:
        Humanity lives on, thankfully free
            Though demented and broken
            Forsaken, exploited and sleepless;
        And I walk on in this very early dawn.

As I come to the front of the old fort –
    Once its steaming, smelly dungeons
    The last habitation this side of the world
    For slaves
    (Those barbaric days of long ago!) –
Three black prison vans arrive
Sweating with dew from their night journey
        From the heart of the country
          To this – their unknown destination.
Slowly, smoothly,
    Like a well-tended engine of torture
    In its first unhurried stirrings,
The black gates of the fort swing open;

Muffled guard voices give the okay
The sweating vans move forward inexorably –
        One, next, then next –
    And vanish into the gaping gateway,
    Merging with the blackness within.
The gates swing shut.

But I have seen them,
I have seen the men huddled within the vans
        Unmistakable;
And I know that they are doomed,
By the odour I know:
        Odour of mildewed maize-cobs
                That farmers heap away in damp corners
                To await the regular ritual of the morning pit!
O God, how could love of fellow-men undo so many?

I slip round to the back of the fort:
        There stands an ancient rock.
The waves roll in, crested as with foaming hate,
        They roll in from the sea
        Rear up menacing
        Break against the Rock
                With a boom and a splash of spray
                Bubbling furiously;
But steady the Rock,
Steady.

This cannot be our last farewell to them,
These men who sought life's justification
    In their battling against injustice;
The cause of Freedom and of Justice is not lost;
The sea destroys
    The sea unknowing also builds.
        Salt of the sea, preserve them;
        Spray from the sea, shower on them grace;
        Rock ancient as time
            Give them of your strength.

Legon, 10 June 1968

An Old Politician to a Novice

This old game to which we are committed –
We must play it
Watching each step
As men do that walk
Sheer mountain paths:

Hitch not your hope to others,
That when they slip
They may tumble to their death
Alone,
While you climb on.

Watch!

Legon, 12 December 1965

When All Is Said and Done

We have heard the owl screeching at the midday sun,
Seen the moonbeam's mystery broken
On prisms of brittle glass.

    When all is said and done
    There's little said and done.

Wood-cutter savouring your axe-fall,
Know you, beyond mere word of ear,
The soul that breathes within the trunk?
Sing softly,
For though limbs be severed
Roots run deep.

When barks decay
Rich mushrooms cluster;
And poison sap dies slow, slowly.

Therefore, son of my mother,
Speak softly to the earth,
Speak softly:

    Let not the poison sap mount again
    Let not the poison leaves sprout afresh.

Legon, 6 March 1966

Deaths: Seventeenth April Nineteen Sixty-Seven

Lt.-Gen. Emmanuel Kwashie Kotoka, Cpt.
Cephas Borkloe, Cpt. Anthony Avevor
and Sgt. Osei Grunshie.
'*And death shall have no dominion*' *Dylan Thomas*

I

This day shall be an oath.
    He that shall name this day
    Let him do so with reverence;
        Else
    He that shall name this day
    Let him not see another dawn.

The death drum wails through the night
It wails unceasing through the noonday heat:
    Whose son is this
    That comes riding upon the empty palanquin?

He the strong-hearted one –
        Katakyi a okum oson
The brave one that felled the mad elephant,
        Okomfo Barimma Katakyi
Soldier of soldiers,
        Ghana-man Katakyi
First in the ranks of this nation's brave. . . .

    Oh woe woe woe!
    Cry woe this nation
        Whose great men die
        At the hand of her hasty youth;
    And woe this nation's youth
        Who would wrest power
        From their mothers' womb itself.

[53]

A brave soldier of his people
A noble son of this land
A gentle counsellor of his time
        Shot through and through and through
        With a murdering sten –

    Oh woe woe woe!
    Cry woe,
    Waters of the Volta.

A red haze grips the land;
North, south, east and west
    The empty valleys echo
    To the cry of circling vultures,
And the death drum wails
    Wails unceasing through the noonday heat:

    Wails
For a captain and a captain and a sergeant,
Martyrs in arms for their nation's weal –
    Also shot,
        Shot in the neck
            In the stomach
                In the heart
    In defence of their taken pledge;

And so our brave sons die!

    Oh woe woe woe!
    Cry woe,
    Waters of the Pra.

[54]

The land heaves with sorrow,
Unstanched sorrow
    Of a nation gored in the heart.
As never before
This nation mourns –
    Mourns red-rust to the horizon
    Mourns red-rust for the blood
    Of a man of iron
        Dead;
The land weeps blood.

But death shall have no dominion
    Even though we wail and weep
    Because we've lost them,
    And lost him who dared
        Evil days
        When but few would dare;
And never shall be lost the memory of them,
And never his memory
So long as this nation stand;
    Never forgotten the brave sound of his voice
    That dawn in February
        When oppression's bastion fell,
        Broken with the myth
        Of one mortal man's ascendancy;

That dawn in February
    When oppression's bastion fell
    Broken,
    Forever broken with the myth
    Of one mortal's infallible will.

II

Ambition will grasp what it craves
  Though all the world be brought to wrack,
And for thirty tarnished pieces of silver
  One out of twelve will betray a master;

But who can tell us
  What they sought
  When they took you unsuspecting –
    (For the cocks gave no warning,
    Only the baying of the guns that morning) –
Who can tell
  What they sought
  When they nailed you through and through
    With burning lead?
Oh who can tell,
Morning without cock-crow!

Or who can tell us
  How you fell
  When the many-throated gun
  Dug its fangs into you?
Who can tell
  Your shock
  Your cry of anguish
  Your dying prayer
  When you fell –
    Fell for this nation
    You led
    Out of bonded days?
Oh who can tell,
Morning without cock-crow!

And as you lay in the lap of death
Was it smile you smiled
When the good general said
    'All is well
    All is well, and
    He is safe' –
Was it smile you smiled?
    Then what smile,
    What smile
    Of a brave man
    For a nation twice betrayed!

    Oh woe woe woe!
    Cry woe
    Waters of Ankobra.

III

For once
    When this nation rose in the splendour of new birth
    Drawing all men's gaze in wonder
    Like a star of hope,
Ere her banners inscribed with Freedom and Justice
    Were full unfurled,
Ere the songs of joy
    Had faded on the ear
    That ushered her to her place
    In the councils of the world,
This nation was betrayed:

Not by enemy action conceived from without
Nor by inadvertent error of good-intentioned men,
    But
By her own people's greed for pelf and pomp,
Their spinelessness that would sacrifice
Truth and principle for expedient compromise –
    Virtue perchance in former times
    Assuring peace of mind and simple amity,
    Now no less than vice ingrained –
Destroyer of noble pride
Death of honour and all conscience.

Thus first,
    Preferring brazen-mouthed folly to soft-spoken wisdom,
    Preferring vain adulation to the life examined,
    Preferring cowardly self-interest to courage
        That would dare the devil
        In name of honesty and conscience,
Thus first
    Her own sons and daughters betrayed this nation
    Betraying
    The trust of the world
    The hope of men centuries oppressed.

Nor lacked this nation alien admirers
    Clarion-tongued like the worst of her children
    Who sang paeans to her apeing antics,
        As she strove to outbid
        Her mentors of the east
    In subversion of
        All liberty
        All human dignity;

The while her chosen in leadership,
      Abetted by the led,
      Wallowed like swine
      In the rising muck of corruption
          And carnal cupidity.

But then you came
      White flame shot from the mystic centre,
      Cleansing,
You came
      Fresh wind sprung from the ends of the world,
      Cleansing,
You came
      Chaste fountain fed from the wells of heaven,
Suddenly you came,
      Long awaited answer to the prayers of good men.

And now the death drum wails,
Wails unceasing through the night
Wails inconsolable through the noonday heat
Wails for a nation a second time betrayed
      By the hand of thoughtless youth.

      Oh woe woe woe!
      Cry woe,
      Waters of Tano.

IV

But we know,
We know that even in death
    Your spirit goes unconquered,
We know that the torch you kindled burns undimmed
    To lead our still errant souls back
    To liberty and self-respect.

For look –
    From across the northern plains
    See now the shepherds and the cattle-men come
    Leading their firstlings of the year
    In silent homage,
    In sacrificial thanksgiving
        For your noble life
        Given this nation by the gods,
        Though but briefly,
        To bring new hope to a people
        In distress.

To the south look –
    Over the golden sands
    See them approach:
    Giant-torsoed men of the sea
    Shaggy-loined
    Seasoned in the salt of many storms,
    In full-throated song they come
        Bringing their meed of the ocean's harvest
    In solemn thanksgiving
        For dignity by you restored
        To a people once steeped
        In dishonour.

Look, from east and west and the middle regions
        See them converge,
        From hilly fastnesses, forests inaccessible,
        From farms and homesteads far-flung
        They come in teeming thousands –
        Offspring of a once warrior people
        Keener than quills of the porcupine,
        Thousands –
        They come
        Bringing the fruits of their earth labour
        In abundant thanksgiving
                For truth by you unchained,
                For conscience once again enstooled.

And as we gather at your shrine
This fervent prayer we raise:
        That
        Out of your blood untimely spilled
        We the people of this land
                May grow new muscle,
        Out of your loss and our sorrow
                Draw strength and courage
        To uphold truth and liberty, always,
        To dare all wrong, whenever, to its knees.

Therefore, brave hero,
And you three, companions in arms,

Wherever you walk
        Go well;
If you must speak of us.
        Speak only good of us,
        Though undeserving;
If you sleep
        Sleep in peace.

Take our condolences:

        Damirifa!
        Damirifa!
        Damirifa due!

Legon, 19 April 1968

Two Views from the Window

I am looking through the window
    At the soldiers marching past.
They are singing, lustily
      About a man with a penis like a cannon
      And a woman who. . . .
But no matter: the songs may be obscene
But everybody is happy, today being anniversary,
And that's all that matters, come to think of it.

The sidewalks are jammed.
The people are cheering the soldiers,
Women spreading their cloth on the tarmac
    For the heroes to march on;
And the men too –
      Even those who cursed bitterly that day
      Because their picnic had been so abruptly stopped –
They are all cheering wildly.
This is the anniversary of the revolution.

A-a-ah! Here comes the commander,
    Riding on his jeep.
He is waving to us
He is waving to everybody,
And they are wild, really wild – cheering!
      You can hear them, can't you?
What a wonderful day!
And what a fine man the commander!
He is a fine man,
    Honest, brave and modest;
Long live the commander!
He's cut just right for the presidency,
    Don't you think?
Yes, we'll make him president,
Long live the commander!

    [63]

All this was only a year ago.
The columns of marching soldiers
    The cheering crowds
        The banners and bunting. . . .
You wouldn't believe it, only a year ago.
But what a year!
    Because during this year we –
    Well, to cut a long story short,
    We went civilian.

And today is anniversary day again
And I am looking through the window.
    No soldiers march along the streets
    No obscene songs
        About a man with a member like. . . .
But no matter;
Let us rejoice, everybody who can,
For that's all that matters, come to think of it.

The crowds are out again.
Thousands of men on the sidewalks,
And the office windows jammed to the top-most floors –
    White-shirted office clerks cheering!
And the women in the streets
    As usual,
    This time demanding redress,
    Proscription of all who took part in
        The exercise that turned into the operation
        That put a stop to the picnic!
Fat-bottomed women, over-dressed and be-powdered,
    Screaming termagants.

I assure you,
   Whoever writes the future history of this land
   will deserve a lynching if he underestimates the
   contribution of our women to the development of
   political consciousness and the establishment
   of the State!

To tell the truth
There has been another revolution, man,
And this is a demonstration
   Of the masses,
   Seething mile upon mile of them.
Look now who comes riding on a jeep, waving to us –
   Not old Moke?!
I tell you, man,
   The old gang's all here!
      'Forward ever backward never'
      'Beep-beep-beep, wɔbɛkɔ assembly'
      'There is victory for us'
      'Down with the opposition' . . . .
And the people are wild, really wild –
Cheering and cheering from the windows;
What a wonderful day!
What a really wonderful day!
As for the commander –
Well, to cut a long story short,
   We went civilian!
   And friends still in touch with him say he is
   Convalescing from the shock:
   As everybody knows,
      He lost the elections to Kwame *in absentia!*

And now the people want their old messiah back.

In parliament tonight they are debating a new bill
        introduced by one of our veteran politicians,
        a man they locked up the day the picnic was
        interrupted.
                (Apart from the big part he had played helping
                to build up the old party on foundations of
                unquestionable infallibility, and his contribution
                to the formulation and operation of the Detention
                Act, he had at one time been master of the revels,
                which meant power to sink millions of our money
                into champagne and caviar and things of that
                sort. He also had been found by a Commission of
                Enquiry to be heavily involved in. . . . But why
                should I bother good citizens with facts everybody
                knows?)
        It is an interesting bill, to say the least.
        Tonight is the final reading,
        And by all accounts it is going to go through
        Without opposition.
                . . . Abolition of all political elections . . .
                Substitution of the Central Committee for the
                        Cabinet . . .
                Presidential prerogatives in all matters judicial . . .
                      Infallibility of the party . . .
                Life tenure of the presidency . . .
                      Etc., etc., etc.
The new deal is in,
And we are back where we were interrupted –
In the middle of the picnic.

This is a big demonstration, man,
And the cheering is deafening!
I see some chiefs over there, on the sidewalk;
The crowd is giving them a tough time,
Pressing them into a corner, pressing;
And they look bewildered;
  But that's nothing new: Chiefs?
  They have been bewildered these fifty years and more
  Except, of course,
  Where they've seen a clear advantage to themselves,
  Then they've acted with decision
  As in this revolution.
  These bewildered chiefs are the few without guts;
  All the others defected long ago
  To the side of the majority in parliament:
  That's where the cedis are!

I do not see any civil servants in the crush.
Poor devils,
  Their picnic is over, as they very well know,
  And they are *back* at the wheel,
  Obediently and faithfully steering the old ship
   To perdition!

As to the intellectuals –
Well, again the same old story:
  The smart lawyers among them
   Quickly diagnosed the new developments,
   And are calmly piling it up in the banks
   While the going is good,
   In the name of the Law and the Constitution;

A few of the university ones
   Got themselves professorships abroad
   For their learned analyses
   Of the many things that went wrong;
Some, like the chiefs,
   Threw in their lot with the new majority
      in parliament,
   And are earning quite decent salaries
   And a growing reputation
   As oracles of the new deal;

Others, the largest percentage naturally,
   No less milky in the liver
   Than any nine hundred and ninety-nine
   Out of a thousand men,
   Are quietly towing the line
      For dear academic comfort
      And a well-earned superannuation;
Of those remaining,
   Some are gone stark mad,
   While the final few, though sane,
   Admit that they are impotent;
   Which, in a situation like the present,
      Would be natural
   Even if they carried cannon between their legs!

Legon, 1 June 1968

The Return of the Multi-Messiah

*(There have been more multi-messiahs in history
than one, and the latest manifestation was here)*

For a year and a day
He lay waiting, bile-crazed,
In exile.

The coming and going of the seasons –
      Cleansing sun and rain,
      Chill August breezes,
      Searching harmattan
            cracking the earth and singeing the grass,
      And the moon
            swinging lean and fat
            among her thousand stars . . .
They changed him not.

Vampire bug
He waited
Sapless yet alive,
Eyes upon the heel of fate's
Pendulum;
Time-teller, yet
Silent
As a secret heart.

Then
He roused himself
To return.

(O skeletal vision of anarchy!
What can measure the tenacity
The tremendous vitality of a creature
Vengeance-purposed,
Power-demented,
      Flesh and bone and brain
      All fused in the beating of
      One satanic motivation?
Not the hand of all the gods of heaven and earth
Nor libations to the gentle dead,
Till of its own accord its force he spent.)

But rejoice you not
    Secret disciples,
For the arm of the multi-messiah falls
    Heavy
    On all men alike;
Neither *you* weep
    Good people,
For life shall triumph

    Even though the multi-messiah returns
    To destroy.

Legon, 21 April 1967

University Franchise Day

In an album
    Dating back to those days
    That I still keep among my things
I found today
    A snapshot
        Of the four organizers,
Another
        Of myself upon the platform,
          Behind the microphone.

There were many of us that day
    I remember,
    Though who each was precisely
        Only a faint memory remains.

We were the saviours in grooming –
The chosen
        We claimed,
    To free this nation then emerging
        From the clutches of cheating imperialists,
    To save her
        From the wreck of a toppling empire.

For tools
    No more than books we had,
    And the will to make a noise!

Fellows
Who most of us
        Had little to recommend us:
No pre-eminence in intelligence
        Let alone imagination,
Not supremely industrious,
Weak-kneed if it came to fighting
        For a principle,
Muddle-headed in execution,
Itching fingers for the Union's purse.

But youth was on our side,
And how we shouted
        For our franchise! –
We who knew not
        Merit
                from
        Sharp dishonesty
                In the conduct of *our* elections,
                In the government of *our* Union;
        Nor cared,
        Most of us.

I hear we now are
        Principal secretaries, some –
                See their long procession come;
        Others ambassadors
        Learned professors
        Heads of corporations;

Erstwhile Cabinet ministers
And leading parliamentarians:
    The whole key lot of public positions.
    Yet in what better
      Than the first man along that weedy footpath
      Home from farm?
    Enlightened stealing, perhaps,
    And vulgar squandermania.

Is it wonder then that
After one score years and one
    The people's cry rises so high in despair,
    The state near rudderless
      All but wrecked?

How our foreign tutors then
    Smiling encouragement
Must have contemned in heart
    Our speeches!

But did they indeed?
For there was hope then –
    At every corner's turning
    On every mother's brow
    In every toddler's wailing.

And what hope betrayed
    Hopelessly –
    By us?

Nairobi, 1 November 1972

[73]

Still at Large

Freedom's guardians
Torch-bearers of the new Africa!
So the world hailed us
So we willed ourselves believe.

Then came the time
We set over ourselves
        The Party Infallible:
        Guardians insatiable of power,
        Ravenous as dogs.

        They trampled
Freedom underfoot;
        They tore to shreds
The sinews of the nation;
What they could of her flesh
Guzzled away,
Licking the skeleton clean;
What they could not
        In sweeping disdain tossed northwards
            To fall under Matterhorn's snowy cap
            Where
            Frozen in ice-bound vaults,
            To await exhumation
        When *their* lean days struck.

The torch we bore
        Snuffed out –
The myth it always was!
        And we the bearers?
        In muddled disarray –
        The mob we always were!

But listen:
    The dogs barking,
    Still at large
        Despite the havoc done;
    Unchained
        Their crimes condoned,
    Still at large
        Despite our hungry dispossessed,
    Still at large!

Nairobi, 31 October 1972

The Vision: Ad Gloriam Africanam

One fateful midnight hour
In a vision,
  Across a stately sky all black, serene,
He saw –
    A shooting star,
    Himself riding
    Astride its incandescent tail
      Ad gloriam Africanam.
The seventh day to the minute
    A coup flashed across the land:
      The newest head of state was born.

    Mar the pattern
    Snarl the thread:
  What the goat can weave
  The colobus too can weave –
    And better!

The thunder that announced his birth
Still echoes
Down the hushed corridors of ousted power.

    Seize the shuttle
    Break the loom:
  What the goat can weave
  The colobus too can weave –
    No better!

Seven promised years
Of plenty for all. . . .
  We not his tribesmen
  Still gaze
    At his bemedalled image on the wall;
  Groaning stomachs
  Severed hands
  Tongues tied
   But still in hope:
    Manna from the louring skies?

Nairobi, 17 May 1972

And All Our Lights Were Burning Bright

That evening
Mumbi came and sat at my feet
Fear in her distant eyes.
    My husband,
    They have been on the air again,
        She said;
    They say you have been talking.

    Power reared on treason shall not last,
        I said;
    This well they know
    And all the people they would rule.
    But woe the man who dares
    To speak it out aloud,
        I said;
    Silence in our time is more than golden.

That middle of the night later
No heavy knocking on the door
Presaged their coming –
Our faithful servant-man had seen to that:
Sudden from my dazed pillow
Only the men's faces towering grim,
And their officer's stern voice
Which said:
    You are to come with us, sir.

Mumbi was brave
That morning past midnight
As I stepped into the Land-Rover,
The men's bayonets at my back.
Last view
From the cramped interior of my bristling cage
As we drove into the darkness:
       The front-room door was still wide open
       Mumbi was standing on the stoep outside
       And all our lights were burning bright.

Nairobi, 17 December 1973

Gently Fall the Leaves

TO YAA-JO, COBBIE AND KWEKU

Echoes from the sea and the stars
And children's voices singing. . . .

If I reach forward
    My roosters die;
Behind me
    Roosters upon rafters
    My roosters strangled,
    Cobwebs between rafters.

Let my eyes be filled with cowries
Let my sleep be sound and endless;
Peace to them gone into the mists
Peace to them that arrive
    Upon the waves and sands.

My young ones,
If you hear talk of
    Torture in the morning,
    Men tortured at seed-time
        that would not yield to expediency,
Do not bend double
Do not bend backwards:
    The evening shall be yours, its song,
    And harvest-time laughter –
        So your courage keeps blazing pure!

Echoes from the sea and the stars
And children's voices singing. . . .

    Gently fall the leaves
    Silently the dust.

Legon, 20 March 1968

[80]

3

SOMETHING IN THE SKY

Night Thoughts

The night has many voices.
I have heard them
When I have lain yawning
All night, waiting for sleep.
And when sleep has come
And I have turned and tossed until,
Sleep-weary, I have yawned myself to waking again,
The voices have been there,
The voices of the night speaking.

Sometimes I have felt myself growing old
Lying there in my faded pyjamas,
Listening to the cricket in the grass.
The cricket is always there
Jingling through the night.
And the mosquito comes singing very close
And vexes me rubbing his feet on the tip of my nose;
And the late cars keep droning home
One at a time, always one at a time,
While the Smith clock ticks.

Faraway voices crowd in upon me
From worlds only the mind in delirium comprehends:
Footsteps insistent
Endlessly tramping
Beating beating beating
Through my burning brow;
And always in the same direction:
Tramping to the pits where they mine the gold –
Soft gold, easy gold, gold of the mine.
The call of the mine is very strong,
Few can resist the call of the mine.

[83]

Sometimes I have felt myself growing old
Lying there in my faded pyjamas,
Tossing to the sound of the tramping feet;
And for my pillow – a hard volume,
Some dead poet's forgotten agonies,
A worn-out volume of ballads and songs.

And in the mining pits men laugh
Picking nuggets to jazz and brass-band,
While the women wash the nuggets,
Stringing them and dangling them
Till their eyes reflect the golden glitter
And their bodies sway to rhythm.

The men dance in a ritual of desire.
From smoke-tumid lungs their laughter rises
Warm,
Expanding and rebounding
Till the pits resound and echo;
And their bodies sway to rhythm.

In the mining pits men laugh
Till,
Victims of mine sickness,
They find they cannot laugh no more;

Then
They come creeping back
Broken and weary,
Seeking somewhere to rest –
Anywhere, if only for a while
They may lay their throbbing heads
On some pillow no matter how hard,
Perhaps a worn-out volume of ballads and songs;
For in the pits there are no pillows.

Picking nuggets in the mines,
Lying yawning in the darkness,
There is no rest;
Only as
Unawares
We catch ourselves at a standstill
When we have been listening to
    The voice of the flute
    Quiet and mellow
    Beneath and through the jazz and brass-band,
Or when we have been whispering scraps
From some worn-out volume of ballads and songs,
Scraps we cherish for the meaning they seem to make.
Beyond this, and up to it,
Only
Dingy rooms and failing lights,
Watering eyes and aching spines,
Shrieks of laughter mocking everything.

South West, November 1952
Nairobi, 8 June 1973

[85]

The Gene

Time went to dine with Science
And rose reeling from draughts of human blood,
A crimson ulcer flaming on his chromosome.

This is the hush hour before the holocaust:
You
And me
And you –
Victims patiently waiting
To be slaughtered upon decadent altars
For worlds already septic in the womb.

Who will redeem the future?
Time is a hermaphrodite,
And the ulcer burns crimson on her chromosome.

January 1953

Clay

Early I fell among potters,
And so like feather were their fingers.
I was the clay, they the makers,
And as the wheel turned so I turned.
Oh, I loved their soft caresses,
Their sleekness, -form- and beauty-giving fingers.

Noon . . .
I dozed . . .
But no repose.
A figure came and went,
Haunting me;
It was a spectre of myself
Touched grey . . . trembling grey;
And it spoke:
    'Feel within your clay, take thought:
    Drinking mug, flower vase,
    Belly, spout or handle?
    The end is yours.'

I am sleep-forsaken.
Still I lie and with the wheel turn;
But there is come a tension in my clay,
A toughness unyielding, thews and sinews.
Clay must yield, or stay; but not mine:
My clay has lost plasticity,
It bounces like steel springs.

November 1952

Mother to an Ungrateful Son

If your teeth turn yellow
You do not knock them out;
They're yours,
They're what you've got to lick!

    Nine painful turns of the moon
    I was the dam,
    These the groins that strained,
    Holding back life's waters
    So you may live in growth,
    Even as the tadpole lives in its changes
    When the hidden ponds swell with rain.

    Fifteen more suckling turns
    These withered dugs you shrink to see
    Ran like sluices with brimming milk
    To nurse you,
    Give you sense and more than sense:
        Mother-love –
        That pull of currents inward
        To the still whirlpool heart
        Of a dam filled to bursting
        With swirling life.

And since?
I've counted toes and fingers with the
Years,
Watching over you,
Till I must begin all over again;
Have scraped and scratched
With these fingers you dare not clasp
Lest you prick your tender palm,
So you may grow
In the ease of new found ways,
The pride of alien rags.

What now?
Where the calm after the rain,
The joy hoped for?
      Only this, this
      Scorn,
Because you dare not lick old golden teeth!

April 1960
Nairobi, March 1973

The Avenue: N.Y. City

Shapes of men
  Caught-riveted spread-eagle-wise
  In toils of steel girders
  Scraping skywards into the sun.

Souls of men
  Trapped-lost blind-mouse-like
  In a maze of asphalt channels,
  Rat-racing round the clock.

Man
  The city builder
Man
  The world girdler
Man
  The rejected prayer.

  N.Y., 1960

The Old Sea Chain

At the end of this slipway,
Beyond the foaming breakers,
The old sailing ships used to rest
Preening their white wings in the breeze
As they waited for their cargo.

Look now, how the green seaweed
Covers all the slipway!

Now feel,
Feel with the sole of your infant feet
The fierce dragon rock beneath the silken weed,
Teeth-of-dragon rock stained red-brown
As with ancient blood –
Blood not all the waters of the sea can wash away.

Then look across the ocean;
Look beyond the breakers,
Far out beyond the curve
Of meeting sky and ocean,
And tell me what you see.

Nothing?

Yet in those ancestral days
There was a chain –
A chain of flesh and iron wrought;
And it held beyond this slipway,
Reaching out to sea
Far, far beyond the curve
Of meeting sky and ocean,
On to the other side of the Atlantic.

1962

[91]

To Poets

One heard talk yesterday of
Words your trade.
Oh woe the day!

Touch you the conscience of men?

    Then words not your trade
    But
    The streaking arrow-head homing,
    Truth the bow behind it.

    Then not
    By twists and turns vocabular
    Shirking the hub of meaning
    For the dubious circumference:
    Mark you
    The word centrifugal.

Shape you our world anew?

    Then words not your trade
    But
    The hammer and the anvil,
    Truth the arm that fashions.

    Then not
    With words ambivalent
    Concealing intellectual uncertainties –
    Shift of politic manipulators:
    Mark you
    The word iscariot.

Take you thought again,
You
Who would plumb the deeps of life
With weighted words.

Dare you speak of prophecies?

    Then mark
    The word
    Upright and naked,
    Pulsing with phallic power –
    The word immaculate.

    The word
    The flesh bands and the cavity and the liquessence
    Of your heart,
    Mind-beat,
    The word immaculate.

Words
Not
Your trade,
Not
Our trade.

    Legon, 8 March 1965
    Nairobi, 4 April 1973

Till 15
I laid up treasure in heaven!
Early christened in the fold – pen A;
Later schooled in the fold – pen Z;
All this despite those worship-day delinquencies
Which we paid for next day
Those hellish Monday mornings in school.

Winnowing of the chaff from the grain
Counting of the goats from the sheep,
White sheep in shining robes
Flapping angelic wings
Those hellish Monday mornings in school.

And the anguish of those sheep faces
Denying you
Outstaring you
Till you dumbly fell in line
    Heart heavy
With others like you condemned
    Heart aching
To await the teacher's rough grab
    Heart pounding
Then the lightning rod
And the agony of the screaming void
Those hellish Monday mornings in school.

Then the dazed re-awakening
Cold in sweat
Alone at your desk in the corner
    Hating

The splinter boring deep into your heart
        Hating
And the angelic sheep faces still denying you
Those hellish Monday mornings in school.

O Jerusalem Hill,
Where now your sons and daughters
The holy ones bleached in the blood of the lamb,
And your champing pedagogues –
Wielders of God's will
        By betrayal and the rod?

Christ!
The wrong we do
The wrong your ministers
Condition us to do
        In name of piety –
        Goodness! –
Even so innocently fresh from the womb.

But deal gently with us all
You
Black Fire-Breasted Rock at the still heart of the fountain,
Deal gently with us all
Mother
For we know not what we do.

Thus early were we broken in;
And as the years passed over
We took and ate,
Almost in second nature,
Steadily building up credit in heaven
Till 15.

10 March 1965

[95]

Dirge to my Father

died 9 November 1936
buried 11 November 1936

Odomankoma Nyame She is one
Therefore let me not deify the dead.

> *Yet hug him gently to your breast*
> *Good earth, Mother of us all,*
> *Hug him gently*
> *For from his loins I sprang.*

At six in the wake of the storm
The big heart stopped.
Ninth twilight of the eleventh moon
Twilight at twelve and a half
The long twilight of orphaned youth.

> *Hug him gently to your breast*
> *For from his loins I sprang.*

At eleven on the day of remembrance
    (Paper poppies for remembrance)
They let him down to his sudden rest,
And we to walk abroad
His words on our heart: Be men, sons of a man.

> *Hug him gently to your breast*
> *For from his loins I sprang.*

And oh, the majesty of him recalled
    (Even now, well nigh thirty harmattans after)
The sheer towering majesty of him
Inspiring love and fear!

Master of many wives
  Whose countless sons he fathered;
Wise spokesman of his people
  Who answer to the call of the waiting crab
  (The thirty that vanquished a thousand);
Strong man of the one word,
Otwi ab'ma: handsome as the leopard!

  Hug him gently to your breast
  For from his loins I sprang.

And you, my mother of the tears
  And my sustainer through the years,
  Single among all women
  Rare bead that speaks not,
    They that will burn you, be not burned,
    Let not your heart be troubled.

  Legon, 2 April 1965

In Memory of a Poet

And what shall we remember him by?
    Not by the high throne of office
        he sat on,
    Not his golden mention in the scrolls
        of the nation's great,
    Neither power, which he never knew,
        to summon or dismiss,
    Nor his quarried likeness set
        in the centre of the Square.

What then shall we remember him by?
    Children sleep-drunk around the dying fire,
    Old folk weary with their life,
    Workmen home from days of dusty toil, and
    Lovers cloistered in the stillness
        of moonlit shadows –
    All who listened to his voice,
        Spell-bound,

We shall remember him
    By the truths he dared to speak,
    The songs of hope he gave us
        To sing.

Legon, 22 September 1967

An Un-African Breakfast

(Spoken to free guitar accompaniment)

So here I am this morning
Early in the kitchen.

The aroma of fresh coffee on the boil,
     Nose-filling aroma of good fresh coffee
        on the boil;
     And this kitchen is good to be in
     And good to hear the browning water
        babble-bubbling inside the glass trap
        head of the percolator;
And the good wife still asleep in her vono bed
Dreaming good dreams, I hope,
Of me!

All night the tummy hasn't been well,
     Running like it wanted nothing more
        to do with me for eating what I
        do not know –
     All night a running tummy;
     Till at last out of weariness
I drop into oblivion between 4 and 5
Quite unknowing –
     Deep oblivion
     Sweet as feathers. . . .

Then crash out of nowhere
The white day comes bursting in
     Through frosted louvres. . . .

And it's good to be alive!

Good indeed to be alive,
    So thank we God
        For everything
        And the myriad sparrows
        Chirruping in the fresh morning sun outside
        While the percolator bubbles.

And here a loaf of bread
And there a jar of marmalade
And sugar for the dreaming wife
And milk just turned out of its blue tin
        now rolling
            on its back
        like a cat,
And there the frying-pan on the gas cooker
    And two eggs spluttering away –
    Yolk of golden egg with garnishing of
        onion and new-cut pepper green and
        winking red,
And a little salt
    A little salt. . . .

    Oh damn!
    A hot speck of spitting oil near got me
    In the eye

    Yes reader
    What d'you say?

Oh, mustn't I?
    Mustn't drink good coffee in the
        morning,
    Mustn't eat good bread and marmalade
        for breakfast,
    Mustn't fry eggs over a gas cooker
        While my good wife
        Still lies dreaming,
And mustn't read books, I suppose,
Nor write poetry,
    Because –
What d'you say?
    Because
    Not African!

But listen
The radio in my sitting-room
(I should have told you of the radio):
Listen –
    Drum sounds *on 15 megacycles*
    Signalling the new day in Africa,
    Pop sounds
    Calling the waking continent
    To the Breakfast Show,
    Many-tongued voices
    Daring all men everywhere
        To breathe in the dawn-fresh winds
        Blowing across a changing world.

And the warrior chieftains pass on
And the beaded maidens dance away
And we sit by the running waters
And sigh for an innocence that is gone.

But here –
        The eggs are done;

And still it's good to be alive!
And though I cannot whistle out loud
I know there is joy
        Bubbling like coffee inside me,
Sweet aromatic joy of
        Of being alive,
        So thank we god
                        For everything
                        And the myriad sparrows
                        Chirruping in the fresh morning sun outside
                        While the percolator babbles,
        And I feel coming alive within me
        The first movement of an un-African poem.

Legon, 2 July 1967

A Man Breaking Stones

Let it stand,
Let this house stand
     built with stones
     the labour of my arm;
Let this house stand,
For a man breaking stones
Is a man branded to be forgotten.

Smoked herring heads and
Morsels of kenkey
     eaten from hand to mouth
Is no food for princes;
Yet let me rise,
From the lowliness of this fare
Let my spirit rise.

A rough pallet on the floor
A homely wife to share each night;
But when the stars look down
Let my manhood stand,
In the fecundity of a responding woman
Let my manhood be

Vindicated.

Legon, 8 August 1967

Death of a Mahogany

Year upon year the pride of this forest;
Then
From the sudden skies
One night came the forked fire
And struck.

Here now I stand
Disembowelled
A charred mutilation dropping limbs,
Food for the parasitic new life
Of this teeming jungle.

Ash. Mampong, 1963

The Morning After

You with your dirty mind
You think I committed some juicy sin, don't you?
Because of the title of this poem
Your dirty mind figures
I've gone and committed some sin
    With, preferably for you,
        Some maiden.
But I've done nothing of the sort
(And anyway I don't care about your *sin*)
My friend with the dirty mind.

But if you want to know –
It's simply that I feel so absolutely pointless
    After all the frantic effort last night
    And right on into the big small hours of today,
        Everybody driving it so hard
        Trying to enjoy themselves,
            Swilling dozens of
                beer
                and gin
                and whisky
                and campari
                and oh – the lot,
            Without head or tail;
        Then reeling about like so many
            Tipsy jackanapeses:
            We called it
            good fun
            twist
            and soul
            and high-life
            and hot time calypso!

Only to wake up at eleven in the morning, Sunday,
    (After a seamless sleep, admittedly)
To find that I am back again home
    (How I don't know)
Alone
Separate;
And nothing of the joy and the gaiety
Not a trace of the sensation of togetherness
Or the fine feeling of making profound meaning
    But this insipid recollection of it all!
Such phrenetic grasping after happiness. . . .
        Oh crackers me,
            I wish I were a sea anemone!

Legon, 30 June 1968

Do Not Tell Me, Friend

Do not tell me, friend,
How much your feet itch
To take the footpath
Out of this forest clearing
    Where nothing stirs
    But the leaves protesting
        against the world-ranging wind's
        constant teasing;
    And the weaver birds returning
        for a while to breed in the
        sunset branches
        And off again tomorrow's season;
    And the streaked barn-mouse content to live
        its tremulous days among the husks
        of last year's harvest;
Do not tell me, friend.

Looking into your eyes
I can tell –
    Your yearning for the world beyond,
    Your brave dreams
    Of towns and cities awaiting conquest, yielding
        Their wealth of work
        And exotic women's love
        And acclaim for wondrous deeds
        Never before done by man.
Looking into your eyes
I know.

But I know, too, that once
One young like you
Dreamed like you
And yearned:

The footpath opened out into the road,
The road into the towns,
And thence –
        The wide sea's trackless way,
        The expanding universe above sun-bleached clouds –
To fabulous cities founded on gold.

In the forest clearing
        The weaver birds knew his presence:
        Their querulous cries would stop
        And then begin again
                In salutation
                Of another nature's creature.
        The leaves smelt fresh above him
        And oozed sweet sap beneath his tread;
        And when night came
                The earth breathed upon his rest,
                The stars drew near.

Now –
A ceaseless roar of machines,
        Metal gods
        That acknowledged not his presence
        But demanded endless service;
And disembodied voices flying on the air
        Whirled round and round his ears –
        Incessant din of rumours and alarms;

He sought consolation
    In the arms of one he met
    On his wanderings.
Engulfed within her soft embrace
    He dreamt
    He had found the stillness
        Of the forest clearing he knew;
But the eyes that had beckoned him with their calm
    Suddenly stared back flat and scared:
        In their pupils he glimpsed a horror spreading,
    And all around him –
        Throngs of rest-forsaken humanity.

His feet grew wings;
But perched atop the tallest edifice of all
At last his heart misgave him:
    Though high above the world
        No nearer was he to the stars;
    Miles below him
        Life roared on
        And still there was great stir;
        And men,
        Grown smaller now than mice,
        Raced round, about their narrow business
            Among the debris
            Of a synthetic
            Unsympathetic world.

Legon, 20 May 1968

The Cycle

On the beach –
Burning sand;
    I lie in a jutting rock's shadow
    Musing on the dog that passed this way
        yesterday.

    Thus we subsist
        Scorched by fire;
    End
        Ashes to earth,
        Water to the winds,
            To the green earth
            Receiving mother;
    Commence again
        (With the breaking of the waters)
        Ingesting air.

    And thus full cycle:
Immortality
        In a dog's whitening faeces.

Nairobi, 20 January 1971

Farewell to Laughter

(Thoughts walking along a quiet street in London)

I see you are bewildered
    My daughter
That I who, back home, can laugh
    So big
    The house-roof could blow away,
Now go about subdued to timid whispering
    Daring not laugh at all.

Do not be bewildered.

    Here
Where we have come
Men talk in whispers
    Or must brave the staring disapproval
        of old wives who missed the flight
        to high-class respectability –
        to upper middle-class prosperity;
Neither do men laugh aloud
    Lest the quiet street explode in their face
        with a charge of neighbourly nuisance.

This morning at the zoo
    You heard the lion roar
    And saw the ageing ladies
        smile approvingly
    While their husbands sucked
        contentedly at lollipops.

Here
Where we have come
The natives love the roar of captive lions;
But we
    Not being caged, perhaps,
    Are feared above caged lions.
And as they would hunt down a lion at large
    Even though he roared not
So would they hunt us down
    If we dared raise our voices.

    For here
Men talk in whispers,
And already our colour talks too loud.

London, August 1965

Stereotypes

Five months pregnant
    By a rich haberdasher husband
    Who shuttles away his gentle life
    Between Nairobi and Mombasa
    To make more than enough to keep her happy,
And she says she wants my brother;
Wants him
    Because she would love to feel
    The beat of a black loin
She says,
    The noblest she ever set eyes on.

    What of your husband and your coming son?
Says my brother;
    Oh, forget about them
She says;
    We whites don't mind, you know.

    Not me,
Says my brother nodding in *my* direction;
    I don't want to hurt her ego
He says, controlled and calm;
    Besides I like her husband Tony
    And prefer my own wife Mumbi.

But she is stripping him naked
    With her eyes,
Slovening back low on her side of the sofa;
And she is drivelling inside,
    You can tell by her crossed leg,
                Creamy pink,
    The way it is jigging the sex rhythm. . . .

And me –
Has she no eyes for me,
This lady with coal tar on her brain?
Bless her aching soul
That hardly notices me
       Despite my rich roasted-cocoa –
       Much, much nearer her black desire
       Than my brother's honey-brown could ever come,
       Than she may ever hope to get!

But she is dying
    For the beat of a black loin
She says,
    For the rape of a black stallion
She fervidly conceives, no doubt.

       And her coming son –
       What will he be:
       Red, black, yellow, white
       Or one of those subtler shades between
       That most of us mortals somehow come in?
       And will he too be colour blind
As she,
Lady in search of her black stud?

Nairobi, 21 October 1972

African Mask

Is it anguish that twists
    So tight in tortured folds
        Your muscled brows
        Your bridge
        Your cheeks?
    What anguish then
    And from what heart?
Or fury at some unnamed injustice
    By whom inflicted,
    Rising from what throat
        Without sound,
    Or sound so pitched intense
    My drum of common earth despairs to register
      Its ultra-sonic frequency?
Whatever lies at the centre of your passion,
    Your space-incarnate heart
    Knows not one man's agony
        It seems,
    But a universal woe
    Fathomless as the depths behind
        Your lids
        All human eyes encompassing.

Legon, 27 April 1968

Salute in the Night

On reading *Can Remembered* in *The Classic*,
Vol. 2, No. 4, 1968

It's three in the middle of the night and I'm
    lying in bed reading about
    This man.
And I think to myself he must have had something –
    This man.

A VC 10 suddenly comes to life two miles away at the
    airport
    And the booming waves fill the night
    Brim over
        flooding the world
        rising to a monstrous roar
    Then recede with a drone . . .
Perhaps a direct flight to Johannesburg.

And I am alone again in a silent world
    Alone reading in a world asleep,
So innocently breathing in its sleep
    You wouldn't think
    It could be so cruel to any man –

This man who had something to say that would not
    be listened to,
    and so
He died the day the banning order was served on him.

I am lying in bed
Wide awake
Middle of the night
Cannot sleep.

Now then, listen, *you old bastard*
    (wherever you are):
Though I've never met you beyond a few
    written scraps about you,
Nor will ever possibly come anywhere near
    understanding
    the agony that destroyed
    You,

  I too salute you,
    Because there must have been something
    truly great you had;
And if you ever get round to setting up
    another *house of truth* where you now are,
Be sure I'll be joining you over a *haja*
    one of these days –
    So long as it's not in heaven but some
    better place yet untouched by the
    foul hypocrisy of pious men.

Meantime I salute you,
    Drunken angel with golden wings:
Salute,
    Can *von* Themba.

    Legon, 18 March 1968

Poem

Echoes within words
Signification of words
   Wrestling;
      A poise: black tarn stillness
      But a mount and a plunge there surfaced,
      Skies and deeps;
Strain, then
Sudden give –
   Gasp of meaning!

  Legon, 21 July 1968

Witch

Here are no cauldrons
Nor assignations on blasted heathland
    Stewed in fog and filthy air –
        A fevered Shakespeare's fancy.

Embryo filcher
Your bosom friend me, or dimpled sister
    Loving by day;
Or maybe me, your kindly-eyed aunt –
    No dewlapped, bearded hag but me
    Who gave you suck
    When your mother's milk ran dry.

Straddling beams of light
    I fly,
Fireball huntress searing slumbering
        Mind-sky
      With owl glee;
What protective wall, what talisman
    Withstand my venom-thought lances?

Scan your shadow:
    I sow in the clan my evil will,
    On the scorching tarmac hatch my maggots.

Legon, 13 August 1968

Night Riders of Nairobi

As yet but
   A dream of distant bees –
   A dim sensation of a humming
      Slow blossoming on the horizon . . .
        Subliminal . . .
Then suddenly
     From the ends of sleep
Revving up to a scorching din octaves hot
                   And a spluttering whine —— !

What prowling beast of the night
   Ripping apart
    This city's sleeping womb
   Till mind shudders awake
   To a premature birth of quivering nerves,
   And ears clutch for naked hiding?

Midnight riders!
   Youth helmeted in steel:
   Whence,
     And what the quest
       At such full throttle
   None can tell;

Into the distance they snarl away,
Trailing combustion
   Like a giant fart athwart the midnight silence;
   And oh –
    My heart
     Still convulsed
      At the jolt of the sadistic awakening!

   April 1969

   [120]

Crippled Beggar

The cock that on tip-toe flaunts
  Its flaming-comb challenge at
    recoiling night
Is his undoing,
    Its bugle dawn-call
      His knell of manhood
        Resurrecting each day's gritty agony,
          Each eternal day's humiliation of dusty feet.

In his crippled loin a wild cauldron rages;
But no ring-necked beauty
    Swinging by on heifer hips –
  Not one in a day's milling thousands
    Dare look into his longing eyes,
  Not one
      Dare his kerb-bound hope engage.

Proffered pennies rolling round his broken knees
Stir in his caged heart
  A frustration and an impotence un-named;
But what brief-cased businessman
    Stepping high past
    In straight-limbed pursuit of dollars
      Cares about the hurt in his eyes?
  Not one
      Thieving business-son of a bitch.

Yet someone lit this man's beggared fires!

Odomankoma,*
Hear us on behalf of all helpless men:
    That your hopeful arm may reach down to them,
        Even them that crawl
        In the dirt of our feet.

    Nairobi, 3 April 1971

---

* *Odomankoma*: the creator and sustainer of all life.

Hibiscus

Come with me quickly – look,
      The hibiscus
      Flaming red-vermilion
      In the glorious morning light.
Come closer – look, look:
      Raindrops
      Still sparkling on her petals
      And in her deep, deep heart
      Like a trumpet-well of liquidest crimson,
      Out of which she seems to thrust
      Her pollen-clustered arm, impulsively,
      Feeling with delicate fingers
      For the friendship of the world.
Whence did you distil your radiance,
      Flower so frail yet so robust?
From the sun and the dew
      The air and the earth,
      And the breath of the spirit
      That holds up the sky.

Legon, 22 May 1968

Japhy Ryder: Dharma Bum
TO JACK KEROUAC

There go the dogs again,
I wonder what's the matter this time?

      Oh nothing, my dear;
      Only Zen Lunatic Japhy
      Passing along on human feet,
      His rucksack on his back.

Poor poor Japhy!
It's so chilly dark outside
But warm in here and cosy too;
Shall we ask him in to view with us
And a cup of coffee maybe?

      You may if you fancy, my dear,
      Only – you don't know Japhy.
      His eyes are on the stars
      His feet on snow-bound Matterhorn
      His soul ecstatic in distant Japan
            Sipping tea with old Zen Masters.
      He owns no TV nor a house,
      And the neighbourhood dogs may growl at him
            For coming by on human feet,
      But he's richer-happier far than we, my dear,
            Because
            He's set on his way to the Dharma.

Legon, 20 June 1968

The Bean Garden

TO GEORGE A-W.

Morning or evening,
Could mind cease from pondering
    Your words, George,
    As I pace my little garden
        Alive with spiralling beans
        New-posted in ranks of riotous green?
    Your simple words
    Spoken doubtless in spontaneous levity,
    But in imagination more terrifying
        Than towering *Ejuanema*
        Striding over-me-wards
        In five-furlong boots of virgin granite
        To pulverize,
        To annihilate kitten me:
O God, we have pissed in your bean garden!

My little garden
World planted with my ten fingers –
Spiralling heart tendrils: pride and hope. . . .

'Twere a grave offence indeed, George,
Were it so;
For which we still devoutly believe
She would forgive us in her infinite love?
Delusion
To think there holds between us and God
An eternal covenant of malefaction and mercy.

Odomankoma forgive us –
  She who nurses within her flashing breast
  All the lightning of the heavens?
Woeful delusion
  More terrifying
  Than *Ejuanema's* earth-quaking footfall
  Echoing down my kitten heart.

Legon, 19 July 1968

New Year's Day, 1971

This ward where I lie,
These four enamelled grey walls
A mirror in which all things pass
    From womb days and beyond,
        Linking hands with what's yet to come
        In a still, reflected dance of my countless selves;
Sunlight slanting warm and bright
        Across my bed;
Silence all around
        But for the vegetable vendor's call
        Floating tremulous up
        From the far end of the street;
And the nurses, when they come,
    Demure as nuns about their rites,
    Each exercising her precise given hour
        To inject insulined well-being
        Into a system
            Fluctuating
        Between the diabetic poles
            Of orange and of blue.

Here life whittles
        To a round of meditation,
    Simplifies
        To a quintessence of rest between
        Ingestion and defecation;
Here mind unclogs,
Reclusion hones the senses fine,
And the vivid world of little good things
        Long disregarded
    Begins to live again:

Scent of sweet citrus peel in my
    twitching nostrils,
The blood-blown petals of these potted roses
    on my window sill,
Sour acid of half-ripe plums biting
    into my teeth,
These sparkling drops of suspended tap water
    Burgeoning with infinite patience
        Till,
    Suddenly unable to hold up
        their load of light,
    They plunge with a stifled plop
    Into the china basin below;
And outside –
A wheeling flutter of pigeons like torn pages
    Dark against a sun-drenched sky
        propped on cypresses,
    A cloudless perfection of turquoise.

And gently nudging me, gently,
The question unanswerable:
    To arrive at such stillness
    Need one have whirled through life
        Hither
    As on jet wings
        Across so many years of busy-nothing time,
    To reach such calm?

Begun 1 January 1971
Nairobi, 20 April 1971

[128]

Oedipus: Scapegoat

Was it in dudgeon
The gods marked him so damned:

    If born,
    Then first
        A parricide;
    After –
        Crowned benefactor,
            Incestuous husband-son
        To be cast out
            Abominable
            Unclean?

What wanton wield of thunderbolt!

Yet out of torment grew
        Self-knowledge,
And what the gods had not foreseen:
        Daring humility,
That they may learn
        Even on high Olympus
        His inalienable right
            To question battering fate
            To choose
                His own expulsion from the fold:

        Expiation –

    So that we may be cleansed
    The fetor in our soul.

But:
       Unless we identify
          With the sacrificial goat
       In suffering,
       How then shall we be
          Cleansed:
       How deserve the sacrifice,
          Attain to re-generation?

Nairobi, 29 July 1973

The Suicide of Colonel Lavender, D.S.O.

A TV Experience

Long shot:
       Bright cheerful skies
       Beyond a fret of poplar tops
       And birds.

            A sudden crack
            (Off camera)!

       Scattering wings. . . .
Then swivel of the lens
To earth
       To medium shot:
          A patch of common grass
          A prostrate man. . . .
          Colonel Lavender:
              His former martial gait
                  Collapsed,
              The rifle underneath his arm
                  Spent!

Another shot –
Flashback:
       Colonel Lavender, D.S.O.
       A decent man
       Who did his duty
          In loyal service
          To his country and his king:
So much for what the TV compere said –
     The citation
       Sweetening him like fragrant toilet water
          Secure from all suspicion of his part in things.

So do we live in smug acceptance
Of our abettors' image of ouselves!
Not so our sons –
The cocky inquisitors of a younger generation
Launched from our loins
Into the interviewing seat to torture us
     With our past,
Hind-sight being focus-sharpest
For those whom tender years excused from
     Close involvement
     In the ugly messes of our manhood.
So our dear myth is shattered!

And for the Colonel –
What for him after his exposure
Under the multi-million gazes of a saner(?) world,
Except
     The terror
     Of error
       Too late confronted;
     The shock
       Of having been a tool to sordid ends
       For country and for state!
     The loss of faith
       In all

       But welcome self-destruction?

Nairobi, 15 August 1973

The Dance (2)

His eyes rested steady
    On the face of the restless youth.
Then he said:
    Go, my son,
    Look for the place of the Dance.
And when you find it,
        Dance
            To the Drummer:
            He alone has the Tongue;
        Dance
            In the Rhythm:
            It alone can cleanse;
        Dance
            Into *Odomankoma*:
            She alone is Fathomless.

    Go, my son,
    Seek
        The Dance.

Nairobi, 2 April 1972

[133]

There is Something in the Sky

There is something in the sky –
 Let my hand hold it;
 Let but my leading finger feel it:
  Your fullness
   Like silence
   When the buying and the selling
    of the market-place
  Is ended;
  Your mystery –
 Let but the tip of my little finger tingle to
 You,
  Odomankoma.

Nairobi